Parenting Tips Volume 2: Helping Children Play

By Aaron Fields

ISBN: 978-1953-962-60-7

Children learn so much when they're playing

Aaron Fields

It's important for parents to respect the idea of their children playing. In fact, parents and caregivers should take personal interest in their children playing to experience the benefits.

One of the most important things parents and caregivers can do is to encourage children to play and provide them opportunities to learn. Keep in mind, as children grow, their play changes. Here is a brief look at different things children play with at different ages.

From birth to age one, children like to play peek-a-boo, hide and seek, games with sounds, rattles, and even mirrors.

From age one to two, children like to play with blocks, push and pull toys, pots and pans, music boxes and even shape sorters.

From age two to three, children love dressing up, climbing games and even wheeled vehicles.

From age three to four, children love bubbles, puppets and even books.

From age four to five, children love board games, toy
cameras, and even musical instruments.

From ages five to seven, children love dolls, ball games, and even craft materials.

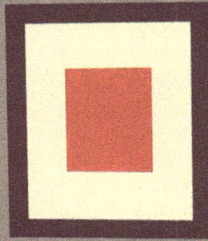

From ages seven to twelve, children love to play sports, card games, and even board games.

Remember this is not a complete list. Children at each stage enjoy a wide range of play, some involving running, jumping, climbing, and others that call for sitting still.

The important thing for parents is to give their children the opportunity to play what they enjoy and what they will learn from.

Why it's important for children to play?

Helping children learn how to play is important for their overall development. Playing creates imagination, creativity, and problem-solving skills. Playing allows children to explore their environment and express themselves in a unique way. It also promotes social skills, as children learn to share, cooperate, and resolve conflicts. In addition to that, play also helps with physical development and enhances coordination and motor skills. By facilitating play, parents, caregivers, and educators give children the chance to grow, learn, and build resilience. This will create a strong foundation for their future.

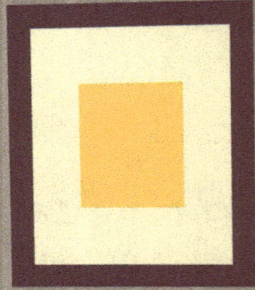

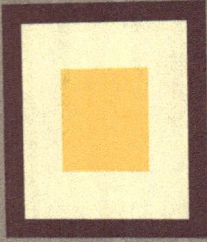

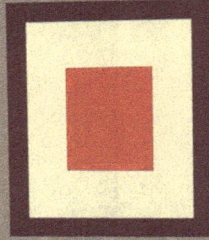

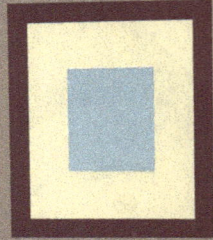